BOYS RULE!

Contents

Tom   Joey

CHAPTER 1

Off to the Country

For Tom and Joey, school holidays are the very best time of the year. These holidays the best friends are off to stay at a dairy farm belonging to a friend of Tom's father. Tom's mother is driving the boys out to the country— they're sitting in the back seat.

Tom "I can't wait to get there!"

Joey "Me neither. Thanks for inviting me. This is going to be cool. I've never been on a farm before. So, when we get there, will we be farmers?"

Tom "Sort of, if we act like Dad's friend, Bill."

Joey "How?"

Tom "Well, Bill walks around with his thumbs stuck in the front of his trousers."

Joey "Well, I can do that."

Tom "And you have to chew a piece of straw at the same time."

Joey "Easy!"

Tom "Also, when you're a farmer there's always stacks of work to do."

Joey "Like what?"

Tom "Well, you've got to milk the cows."

Joey "Why?"

Tom "Um, Earth to Joey—*to get milk.*"

Joey "But you get milk from the shop."

Tom "Yeah, but the milk comes from cows first."

Joey "Oh, I thought that they just made milk in shops."

Tom "No way! Really?"

Joey "Yeah, I've never thought about it. Mum just pours it out of a bottle and I drink it. Hey look, we're here!"

CHAPTER 2

Pink Cows

It seems to have taken forever for
Tom and Joey to arrive at the farm.
Bill welcomes them with a piece of
straw in his mouth. He spits it out
and explains to the boys that they've
arrived just in time to help milk the
cows. Tom and Joey change into their
farm clothes and put on wellingtons
that Bill has given them to wear.

Joey "Have you ever milked a cow?"

Tom "Yeah, I'm an expert!"

Joey "So how many cows have you milked?"

Tom "Well, just one. But it was a really big one."

Joey "Is that it? I don't think that makes you an expert."

Tom "I've looked at a lot of pictures of people milking cows, too."

Joey "So? I've looked at pictures of mountain climbers standing on the top of Mount Everest, but that doesn't mean I'm an expert mountain climber."

Tom "Well, I just know that I'm good at it, that's all."

Bill takes the boys to the milking shed. He tells the farm dogs to go and get the cows. The dogs race off down the field to where the cows are. They bark at the cows and herd them towards the milking shed.

Joey "Farm dogs are really smart."
Tom "Yes, and they're hard workers, too."

Joey "It looks like everybody who lives on a farm has to work really hard."

Joey and Tom watch from the milking shed as the dogs bring the cows in.

Tom "Man, look at them all! Don't they look great? There must be over fifty of them!"

Joey "And they're all different colours."

Tom "Yes. Brown, white, black, black-and-white, all sorts!"

Joey "Where are the pink ones?"

Tom "What? Are you serious?"

Joey doesn't answer Tom.

Tom "You *are* serious!"

Joey "Yeah, well, if there aren't any pink cows, where does pink milk come from?"

Tom "Um, well! The same place as white milk comes from. You just have to put pink colouring in the milk."

Joey "Are you sure?"

Tom "Trust me. Come on now, it's time to be real farmers!"

CHAPTER 3

Time to Milk

The cows slowly amble into the farm yard. "When the cows get into the stalls you have to wash the udders before you put the cups on the teats," Bill tells the boys.

Tom "You know what udders are,
don't you? Look underneath.
That's what they are!"

Joey "Oh. Um, do cows bite?"

Tom "Humans? No. Grass? Yes. You
never know, they might think your
hair is grass and take a chomp."

Joey "Really? Maybe I should put a hat on."

The cows start to move into the milking stalls. Bill shows the boys how to wash the udders and how to place the milking cups onto the teats.

Tom "The teats are the things that are hanging from the udder. They look like thick fingers."

Joey "This is so bizarre!"

The milking pump starts and the dairy shed is suddenly so noisy the boys have to shout to hear each other.

Joey "So, how does the machine work?"

Tom "The machine sucks the milk from the cow, then the milk goes up the pipes and ends up in a big tank over there. It's called a vat."

Joey "Then what happens?"

Tom "A big truck comes and takes the milk away so that it can be put in the shops. Are you ready to put the cups on some cows?"

Joey "Yes! I think."

CHAPTER 4

The Experts

Joey and Tom finish washing the udders with a wet, warm rag and then stop before trying to put the cups on the teats.

Joey "I reckon you should show me how to do it first. You're the expert."

Tom "You chicken?"

Joey "No! Just want to make sure I do it right, that's all."

Tom "Okay. Move away. Let's see."

Bill sees that the boys are having
trouble getting started so he helps
Tom put the cups on the cow.

Tom "See, looks like there's nothing
to it!"

Joey "Yes, right. You couldn't do
it a minute ago. Bill had to come
over and show you again."

Tom "Well, he must've forgotten that I'm an expert farmer."

Joey "Huh! I don't think that you know much more about farming than I do!"

Tom "Um, hello? Who asked where milk comes from? And pink cows! Stand aside. I'll show you. I'm putting these on by myself this time."

Tom bends down and places the cups onto the cow. He proudly grins to himself.

Joey "Hey there, big brown eyes, I hope that doesn't hurt too much. Time for you to let your milk go."

Tom "What are you doing?"

Joey "Talking to the cow—telling her it's time for her to give up her milk."

Tom "I reckon she already knows that."

The boys watch the milk flow through the clear plastic pipes.

Joey "So when do we take the cups off?"

Tom "When you can't see any more milk going through the pipes."

Joey "Gee, you have to be really smart to be a farmer. Hey, what's she doing now? Why is she lifting her tail?"

Tom (smirking) "Um, just move in a little bit closer to her and you'll see why."

CHAPTER 5

Standing in It!

As Joey takes a step towards the
cow, her tail flicks and suddenly
a cow pat gushes from her backside
onto the ground like a fire hose.
Some of it splatters into Joey's
wellingtons. Joey shoots Tom a look
of horror and tries to stop himself
from throwing up. Tom and Bill can't
help breaking out laughing.

Joey "Eewww!! Gross! That's not funny!"

Tom (still laughing) "Yes it is! You should see your face!"

Joey "Look at it! It's all over the place! Maybe we can scoop it up and sell it to people who want to use it in their garden? Cow pats are good for plants aren't they?"

Tom "But they like to call it manure, silly! Hey, since you're standing in it maybe it'll help you grow tall."

Joey "But, I've only got it in one boot. So, if it works I'll have one leg longer than the other!"

Joey joins in the joke and is now laughing with Tom.

Tom "You want me to shovel some into your other boot?"

Joey "Sure, then maybe I'll grow to be a couple of metres tall."

Joey takes his boot off and cleans it. Bill thanks them for their help and the boys take a short cut through a back paddock to the farmhouse, to get something to eat.

Joey "Hey, that's weird. Look! Bill's forgotten to milk one cow. Man, she's huge, and she's running over to us. Tom? Tom?"

Tom (shouting) "Run, Joey! Run! That's not a cow, it's a bull and he's charging us."

Joey and Tom sprint for the fence and throw themselves over it just in the nick of time.

Joey (panting) "Whoa! We nearly died. Unreal! Being on a farm is awesome."

Tom "Um ... You think?"

Tom sees that he has landed in a cow pat and it's all over his jeans. The boys break out laughing.

Tom

BOYS RULE!
Farm Lingo

Joey

dairy The place where the cows are milked. Sometimes it is called a milking shed.

farm dog A dog that lives on a farm. A farm dog helps with rounding up the cattle and sheep.

hay Grass that has grown in a field. The grass gets cut and left to dry. Then it is made into bales and stacked.

teats These look like thick fingers coming out of a cow's udder.

udder The part of a cow that produces milk. It looks like a bag hanging under the cow.

BOYS RULE!
Farm Must-dos

☞ Keep your mouth shut when you walk in a paddock—or else you might swallow a fly.

☞ Always leave gates on a farm as you find them. If you leave them open when they were closed, the cows will get out of the fields.

☞ If you sing in the milking shed, the cows will be really happy and they will give you more milk.

☞ Always treat the farm dog well— it's one of the hardest workers on the farm.

☞ When you are working out in the fields you should always wear a hat. You have to be just as careful in the sun in the country as you do at the beach.

☞ Make sure that you always check the fences to see if there are any holes. If there are, mend them straightaway, or soon you won't have any farm animals left.

☞ You should always be kind to farm animals.

Farm Instant Info

A baby cow is called a calf.

A cat's job on the farm is to catch mice.

You must milk the cows both in the morning and in the afternoon.

To produce milk, a cow must have a calf every year.

A calf stays with its mother for only 48 hours.

A cow has four stomachs.

To make 1 kilogram of butter you need around 22 litres of milk.

Foods made from milk, such as cheese, butter, yoghurt and cream, are known as dairy products.

When cows are milked, special suckers are attached to the teats. The suckers squeeze the milk gently from the cow just like a calf does.

Most cows give about 15 litres of milk per day.

Think Tank

1 If the female is called a cow, what is the male called?

2 Are all cows the same colour?

3 Do you think cows would like to eat meat pies?

4 What do you call a group of cows?

5 How many stomachs do cows have?

6 How many times a day does a cow need to be milked?

7 Do flies like living on farms?

8 Why should you wear wellingtons when you walk around a farm?

Answers

8 You should wear wellingtons in case you step in cow pats.

7 Flies love living on farms.

6 A cow needs to be milked twice a day.

5 A cow has four stomachs.

4 A group of cows is called a herd.

3 No. Cows don't eat meat.

2 No. Cows come in a variety of colours—but not pink!

1 The male is called a bull.

How did you score?

- If you got all 8 answers correct, then you'd be great on a farm. You're a natural!

- If you got 6 answers correct then you don't mind wearing wellingtons and doing just a little work on the farm.

- If you got fewer than 4 answers correct, the best thing for you to do on a farm is feed the chickens.

Felice → ← Phil

Hi Guys!

We have heaps of fun reading and want you to, too. We both believe that being a good reader is really important and so cool.

Try out our suggestions to help you have fun as you read.

At school, why don't you use "On the Farm" as a play and you and your friends can be the actors. Set the scene for your play. Use your imagination and pretend that you are on a dairy farm rounding up the cattle for milking. Perhaps one of the cows is refusing to go into the stall and you have to find a way to make it go in.

So ... have you decided who is going to be Tom and who is going to be Joey? Now, with your friends, read and act out our story in front of the class.

We have a lot of fun when we go to schools and read our stories. After we finish the kids all clap really loudly. When you've finished your play your classmates will do the same. Just remember to look out the window—there might be a talent scout from a television station watching you!

Reading at home is really important and a lot of fun as well.

Take our books home and get someone in your family to read them with you. Maybe they can take on a part in the story.

Remember, reading is a whole lot of fun.

So, as the frog in the local pond would say, Read-it!

And remember, Boys Rule!

BOYS RULE!

Felice

When We Were Kids

Phil

Phil "Have you ever milked a cow?"

Felice "No, but I drink lots of milk! Have you ever milked a cow?"

Phil "Yeah, I've milked heaps of cows. My uncle has a farm and I spent my school holidays working on it."

Felice "Did a cow ever fill your boot?"

Phil "Sure did! And covered my leg as well!"

Felice "Did it make you grow taller?"

Phil "Not sure, but it certainly made the flies happy!"

BOYS RULE!
What a Laugh!

Q Why did the farmer plough his farm with a steamroller?

A He wanted to grow mashed potatoes.

BOYS RULE!

 Gone Fishing

 The Tree House

 Golf Legends

 Camping Out

 Bike Daredevils

 Water Rats

 Skateboard Dudes

 Tennis Ace

 Basketball Buddies

 Secret Agent Heroes

 Wet World

 Rock Star

 Pirate Attack

 Olympic Champions

 Race Car Dreamers

 Hit the Beach

 Rotten School Day

 Halloween Gotcha!

 Battle of the Games

On the Farm

BOYS RULE! books are available from most booksellers.
For mail order information please call Rising Stars
on 01933 443862 or visit www.risingstars-uk.com